AND THE RIVERS THEREOF

AND THE RIVERS THEREOF:

REFLECTIONS ON
RIVERINE IMAGERY
IN THE WRITING
OF JACK KEROUAC

Gregory Stephenson

Felix Culpa Press

Published by Felix Culpa Press
Felix Road, Felixstowe, Suffolk
IP11 7JD

ISBN 978-87-974375-2-0

Grateful acknowledgement is made to
Kevin Ring, editor of *Transit,* in which
a portion of this essay appeared under
the title "For River and Ever."

Cover photo, design & layout by
Birgit Stephenson

For Birgit
toujours

Through the wide wordscape of Jack Kerouac's writing, imagery of rivers wends a course – gliding, rippling, rushing or merely trickling waters of many names bearing in their undercurrents rich sediments of poetic suggestion. "I wrote my first novel at age 11, in a 5 cent notebook," Kerouac once stated, "about an orphan boy running away, floating down a river on a boat." [1] Thereafter, throughout much of Kerouac's prose – from his first published novel to his final printed words – images of rivers make their appearance, multivalent in their resonances, manifold in their layers of meaning.

Rivers as a motif are, of course, recurrent in many oral and written traditions, in the Bible, in classical mythology and throughout literature. (They are central to works by William Wordsworth, Henry David Thoreau, Ralph Waldo Emerson, Mark Twain, Joseph Conrad, Ernest Hemingway, James Joyce, Thomas Wolfe, T.S. Eliot, Annie Dillard and William Least Heat-Moon, to name only a literary few.) Ever moving yet seemingly abiding and unchanging, rivers are rich in archetypal associations and freighted with philo-sophical and spiritual significance, summoning to mind questions of stasis and motion, beginnings and endings, flux and permanence, fertility and destruction, fixedness and freedom, limits and their traversal, and suggesting the stream of time, the mysterious origins and course of human life, the unconscious mind, purity, purification and redemption, the cyclical renewal of life in the natural world, and more. It is my purpose in the following notes to consider certain of the interpretive dimensions of riverine imagery in Jack Kerouac's writing and to assess the role of rivers in the author's oeuvre. I am aware that imagery yields different readings to different readers and I would not presume to pretend that mine is the final word on this motif.

The opening paragraph of Kerouac's debut novel, *The Town and the City* (1950) depicts the Merrimack River, tracing it from its mysterious source in the far north, through its long journey among woods, fields and towns, to its ultimate union with and disappearance into the sea. [2] The novel's narrator links the river's course to human destiny. Young Mickey Martin, we are told, listening from his bed-room window to the rush and roar of the nearby river is moved to ponder "the wellsprings and sources of his own mysterious life." (3) Other residents of the town of Galloway, the narrator apprises us, live their lives, perish and disappear into the earth in concord with "the slow deep pulsing river of life." (4)

Throughout the novel – until the Martin family moves to New York City – the sights and sounds of the Merrimack river form a fixed and steady backdrop to the thoughts and fates of the story's principal characters. As also in the lives and minds of the sundry characters in the novel, the river has its moods. The Merrimack can be wildly – even perilously – fervent when swollen with spring snowmelt and silent and serene through calm summer evenings; its waters can shimmer in sunlight or turn suddenly "dirty and dark" (33) as rain sweeps across them. Twice in the novel, young Mickey Martin – drawn by the spell cast upon him by the river's alluring mystery – vows to voyage upriver in a rowboat, intending to follow the Merrimack to its distant, hidden source, but in both instances he fails to undertake the adventure. Like the mystery of life, the mystery of the river endures, besetting, beckoning, unresolved.

Pawtucket Falls, Merrimack River, Lowell, Mass.

In Jack Kerouac's personal journal for 1949, in which he recorded his progress in writing an early version of *On the Road*, there is an intriguing entry for June 1st of that year. "I'm thinking," Kerouac wrote, "of making *On the Road* a vast story of those I know as well as a study of rain and rivers." [3]

The implication of this statement would seem to be that Kerouac was at this point re-conceiving the nature of the novel he was writing. The rather puzzling reference to "rain and rivers" can be clarified in the light of another journal kept by Kerouac during this same period. Begun in late January of 1949, this latter journal was titled "Rain and Rivers" and consists of accounts of the author's journeys across the United States, descriptions of encounters, musings and observations, all interspersed with notes on various American rivers. [4] Certain of the descriptions he recorded in his "Rain and Rivers" journal were later used – in altered form – in his published writings.

The title of the journal, the detailed notes concerning individual rivers – the origin of their names, their headwaters and courses – together with the author's poetic reflections on them, together suggest that Kerouac intended to employ the image of rivers and the rains that fed them as an underlying, unifying metaphor in the novel he was then writing.

The river as central symbol was still very much on the author's mind when in August of 1950 he completed a version of the novel, re-titled *Gone on the Road*. On the title page of Kerouac's "Private ms. of *Gone on the Road*, Complete First Treatment and with Minor Artistic Corrections," there is an epigraph for the novel in the form of a quotation taken from *Chronicles of the River* by Charles Mad. The citation reads as follows: " 'If you go over the river a second time,' said the explorer to the captain, 'then make it easier for such poor passengers as will have to pass this way, than it was for me, for I have other rivers suffer me.' " [5] I believe that Kerouac's conception of the river image as a potent, central symbol enriching and uniting his narrative survives as a motif in his subsequent, celebrated spontaneous draft of *On the Road*, the version of the novel which eventually became the published text. (Incidentally, I have searched in vain to discover a writer/explorer named Charles Mad and a book or other manuscript titled *Chronicles of the River*. I am half-convinced that Kerouac invented the epigraph and its source. Of course, it may be that the author's source for the quotation is one that is little known.)

In the final published version of *On the Road*, the narrative is both framed by and permeated with imagery of rivers. Already in the opening chapter, the narrator, Sal Paradise, cherishes memories of his boyhood "in those dye-dumps and swim-holes and riversides of Paterson and the Passaic." [6] In the second chapter, embarking on his cross-country journey, he pauses to muse on the Hudson River: "If you drop a rose in the Hudson River at its mysterious source in the Adirondacks, think of all the places it journeys by as it goes out to sea forever –." (10) (A similar image will appear in subsequent writings by Kerouac.) In chapter three, Sal is elated to see "for the first time in my life ... my beloved Mississippi River." (13)

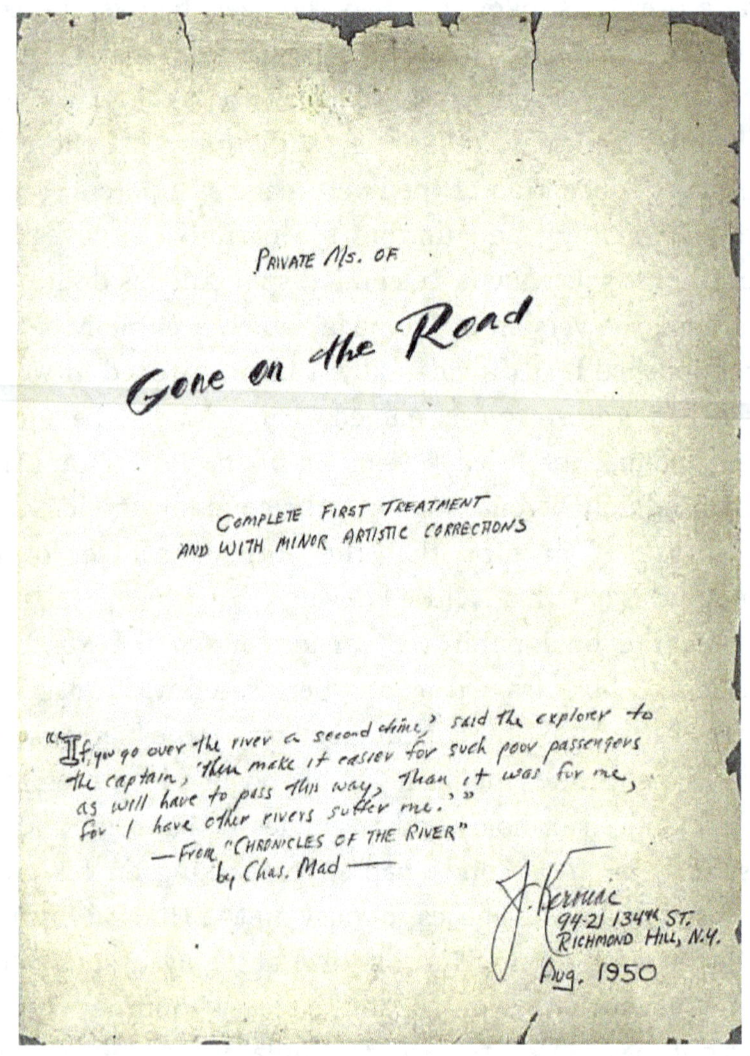

On his return trip eastward across the continent, the narrator stops to take a walk along the Mississippi, contemplating "the logs that come floating from Montana in the north – grand Odyssean logs of our continental dream." (103) Upon a night soon thereafter, he follows the fear-inspiring Susquehanna and ponders other "mournful rivers … the Monogahela, old Potomac and Monocacy." (106)

A further encounter with the Mississippi River occurs near New Orleans, where once more Sal contemplates the river's power and mystery: "the great brown father of waters rolling down from mid-America like the torrent of broken souls – bearing Montana logs and Dakota muds and Iowa vales and things that had drowned in Three Forks, where the secret began in ice." (141) Later, while crossing the Mississippi on a ferry, Sal experiences an epiphany: "as the river poured down from mid-America by starlight I knew, I knew like mad that everything I had ever known and would ever know was One." (147) Bound west again, Sal once more crosses the Mississippi at Port Allen "where the river's all rain and roses," and here he reflects on the river's meaning: "What is the Mississippi River? – a washed clod in the rainy night, a soft plopping from drooping Missouri banks, a dissolving, a riding of the tide down the eternal waterbed, a contribution to brown foams, a voyaging past endless vales and trees and levees, down along, down along, by Memphis, Greenville, Eudora, Vicksburg, Natchez, Port Allen and Port Orleans and Port of the Deltas, by Potash, Venice, and Night's Great Gulf, and out." (156)

Pursuing his travels across America, Sal gazes wistfully at "lovely little tributary rivers flowing softly among the magic trees and greeneries," (236) and glimpses other "enchanted rivers" (238) including the Shenandoah, the Kanawha and the Rio Grande. He honours "the dark and mysterious Ohio" (254) and celebrates a final time "the endless poem" (254) of the Mississippi with its burden of wreckage, detritus and Montana logs. In the final scene of the last chapter of the novel, his journey and his narrative ended, Sal sits alone in reverie and meditation on "an old broken down river pier." (307)

The river motif in *On the Road* augments the riverine imagery deployed in *The Town and the City* and serves to confer perspective, suggesting to the reader a larger, deeper scheme of things within which the lives of the novel's characters take place. Beyond the immediate confusions, sufferings and yearnings of Sal and Dean, their companions and the numerous incidental figures in the novel, there are seen to exist natural cycles and eternal forces, of which rivers are emblematic.

More emphatically than in *The Town and the City*, riverine imagery in the novel also serves to suggest the journey of individual life, from birth through growth to death and union with the ocean of consciousness, the One, from which new life proceeds. Coursing through *On the Road*, rivers evoke a mystic or metaphysical sense of our place in history and eternity and thus act to underpin one of the novel's deepest truths, the sense of life's wonder and mystery, the humbling sense of the infinite.

Through the memory and imagination of Jack Duluoz, the narrator and authorial voice of *Visions of Cody* (written 1951-52, published 1972) the waters of distant rivers purl and murmur: the East River, the Red River, the Roanoke, the Merrimack, the Cimarron, the Missouri, the Fall River, the Hudson, the Potomac, the Neuse, the North River, the Wasatch, the Yellowstone, the Ohio, the Rio Grande, Orinoco and Ventauri. [7] Duluoz laments in one passage his present separation from the river of his childhood and youth: "it's been so long since I've heard the sound of the Merrimack River washing over rocks in the middle of a soft summer's night that I can't make poesies out of it," and yearns to hear again the river's "eternal hush" and "noble tones." (303) The river would seem here to represent to him not only the homey and familiar, but also something lost, something elusive but precious, something that he had hoped to keep.

During the course of a long internal monologue, the narrator envisions an escape from the dominant mores and bland affability of the social world in which he feels stifled, a getaway that would then make possible for him a life of personal autonomy in classic American Huckleberry Finn fashion: floating on a small well-provisioned raft "down a small Indian river that leads to the Mississippi by a series of subsidiary creeks and rivers ... floating down that little Indian river, further and further down into stranger, lighter, greener, ever expanding adventures ... something mad and wild and far far gone from the tangled viney place where you started." (307-308) Clearly, in this passage, the river in imaginative form serves as a vehicle for a dream of self-

Mississippi River

renewal, self-reinvention, a dream of freedom and the expansion of horizons both outer and inner.

Duluoz associates this riverine dream of freedom with a story he wrote at age eleven (see first paragraph above) titled "Mike Explores the Merrimack," wherein "My Mike started in the swamp of the river Merrimack somewhere." (308) To make his way from the "tragic swamp" (308) to the clear swift-moving river current, to be borne away to a fabulous elsewhere. The escape and quest motif of that early literary exercise expresses still the course of an interior journey upon which even now the narrator longs to embark.

Significantly, in the author's description of the much-assailed, "saintly" figure of the musician Lester Young, celebrated here by Kerouac as a modern hero of "mysteries" and "masteries," the ravaged virtuoso jazz-hero is likened to the Mississippi River in an extended simile that honours both the unvanquished man and the mighty river in its mythic grandeur: "Lester is just like the river, the river starts in near Butte, Montana in frozen snow caps (Three Forks) and meanders on down across the states and entire territorial areas of dun bleak land with hawthorn crackling in the sleet, picks up rivers at Bismark, Omaha and St Louis just north, another at Kay-ro, another in Arkansas, Tennessee, comes deluging on New Orleans with muddy news from the land and a roar of subterranean excitement that is like the vibration of the entire land sucked of its gut in mad midnight, fevered, hot, the big mudhole rank clawpole old frogular pawed-soul titanic Mississippi from the North, full of wires, cold wood and horn." (456) The Mississippi River serves here as a touchstone of power and beauty in harmony, a supreme instance of grace and force, against which human achievements must be appraised. To equate the life and music of Lester Young with the Mississippi is for Kerouac acclaim of the highest order.

A darker colouring pervades Kerouac's observations concerning rivers as recorded in his notebooks from 1951-52, assembled for publication by the author in 1957, and published in 2006 as *Book of Sketches*. [8] In one word-sketch, Kerouac records an incident when, gazing down from a railroad bridge into the waters of the Concord River, he sees there below him the carcass of a dead cat. In poetic fashion the piece contrasts the clear sky above and the carcass-bearing river below, the former a metaphor for the "perfect indivisible Unity Forever" (66) of divinity or Supreme Reality; the latter a metaphor for the temporal, material realm of suffering and death, as inhabited by mortal humans and animals. Disguised by the river's benign name is its true essence: discord.

In a similar manner, in a subsequent prose sketch, while contemplating the South Platte River, Kerouac observes with sorrow its defilement by tires, broken glass, bolts, wire, rusty tin cans, oil slicks and sewage pipes. This is what we have so callously and so carelessly done to the pristine beauty of the natural world, the piece proposes, and,

South Platte River, Colo.

by extension – through corresponding inward acts – to the original, inborn purity of our own lives. Along the banks of the South Platte, among the stumps of once sturdy trees, gather broken men whose grim lives are analogous to the stumps: forlorn, diminished men, their once fresh and budding childhood hopes felled by cruel misfortune. "Thru iron tragedies," Kerouac observes, the "sad stream" of the South Platte River, flows on, tainted, burdened but still unyielding in its residual strength. (150)

In common with the South Platte River, the Pajaro River – where in Kerouac's romantic fancy, noble and intrepid cowboys once ranged – is now reduced to the haunt of broken-down winos. (224) And, like the contaminated South Platte of Colorado, the East River – a tidal estuary in New York City – has been befouled, colonized by commerce, its oily waters overrun by barges, tankers and tug boats, its banks, once graced with virgin forest, now overspread by tall office buildings together with a grey, forbidding mental hospital. Hubris and greed, the sketch suggests, have ravaged both the once luxuriantly verdant east coast and the hitherto unspoilt western plains of the New World. In elegiac imagery similar to that in which he described the blighted South Platte, Kerouac notes how now, as he watches: "the river tide swells and is somber below the sad slow parade ..." of shuffling, baffled, ravening humanity. (305) What should have been honoured as a sacramental inter-section between nature and humanity, heaven and earth, has instead been exploited and ill-used.

Through the narrative of *Doctor Sax* (1959) the Merrimac River weaves and winds its way, its waters in their changing moods urging forward the sequence of events that make up the novel. [9] In the course of the story, narrated by young Jackie Duluoz, a boy of 13 or 14 years of age, the Merrimac manifests two contrasting aspects. Most often the river is placid and benign, a soothing sound in the sleeping ears of the townsfolk of Lowell, a source of adventure and pleasure for young boys who swim and dive in its gliding water and sail in small boats carried on its currents. But on occasion the Merrimac turns suddenly wrathful, its lawless waters overflowing their accustomed channel to carry away barns, hen coups and houses, and to drown livestock and hapless, heedless boys.

Already from the earliest description of the river in *Doctor Sax*, the source from which the Merrimac feeds is said to be "snakelike," (8) while during the climactic flood, the narrator sees the river as having "the scaly ululating back of a sea monster, of a Snake." (168) Indeed, the river is subsequently characterized as being the very mouth of the Great Snake of the World, the embodiment in the novel of implacable, all-destructive wickedness. When the river's full fury is unleashed in a spring deluge, the Merrimac is then portrayed as "an unforgettable flow of evil," destroying everything in its path. Yet elsewhere in the novel, when Jackie Duluoz feels oppressed and depressed by the relentless reminders of death that surround him (his dying uncle, a funeral parlor, the gloomy illuminated Stations of the Cross in the Grotto) he remarks that "Everything there was to remind of Death, and nothing in praise of life – except the roar of the humpbacked Merrimac passing over rocks in formations and arms of foam." (125) The river, it will be remembered, often serves as a refuge for the boys, a pleasant, sylvan setting for their recreative activities, a kind of *locus amoenus*. In this role, too, the Merrimac is life-affirming. When the flood begins, Jackie and his companions celebrate the river as a liberator, wanting the flood to "drown the world, the horrible adult routine world," (171) secretly urging the wild river waters to sweep away "everything that ever hated us." (174)

Flood scene, Merrimac River, Lowell, Mass.

The river's dual nature has its parallel in the circadian rhythms of the inhabitants of the town of Lowell, most particularly in the inward life of young Jackie Duluoz, as well as in the lives of his companions. The bright daylight world of Lowell is for the boys one of school and sports, Saturday films and Sunday Mass. Parents, teachers, priests and other adults provide guidance and guardrails. Though boring to the boys, it is a stable world of safety and order. The night-world of Lowell, however, is one of terror, a time when wizards, vampires, spectres, demons and gnomes are given free rein. It is a time when familiar trees and fields, household furnishings and personal effects come alive with menace and malicious intent and all "the underground rumbling horrors of the Lowell night" (44) hold sway in the psyche.

The ravages wrought by the flood upon the city of Lowell might not – in a karmic sense – have been entirely unearned, for the narrator notes with disgust the continual defilement of the Merrimac River with industrial dyes and human sewage. It is further implied that the community (in common with the rest of the nation and the whole of western civilization) has "long lost contact with ... natural phenomena," (180) such as the river. In this regard, early in the novel, the narrator refers to the "floodable river flats" (5) on which whole neighbourhoods of Lowell have been built. If understood and respected, we may infer from this observation, unrestrained forces of nature need not wreak havoc on human communities. But citizens and public officials remain stubbornly, wilfully oblivious to the natural environment they occupy, preoccupied by their particular personal interests, as when the "City Hall golf politicians and clerks who also played golf complained that the river had drowned all the fairways and tees," (180) unable to perceive the triviality of mind and impoverishment of spirit disclosed in their complaint.

Finally, the phallic/snakelike river's irresistible rise and sudden turbulent overflowing would seem to correspond in the novel to the advent of sexual awareness in Jackie Duluoz and his companions, an outward sign of their inward inundation by an irrepressible erotic desire which has been manifesting itself in their lives by random increments. Their new sexual identities thrust upon them by a powerful natural force within their bodies, the boys must now forsake the world of imagination they have inhabited, the world of games and play and adventure. The coming of young manhood means the necessary destruction of childhood. The boys' brief Eden-on-the-Merrimac will be forever lost to them.

The Merrimac River in *Doctor Sax* is a potent, poetic presence, susceptible of many meanings. Comprised of opposition and antithesis, an incongruous convergence of regeneration and death, it is a force beyond human comprehension or control. One senses in the power of the river a hidden teaching, an elusive truth, an atavistic knowledge deeply felt but only dimly discerned.

There is a passage in Kerouac's sprawling assemblage of precepts, parables, poems, reflections, observations, dreams and memories gathered in *Some of the Dharma* that considers the Merrimac as a metaphor for the appearance and disappearance of the created world in the Divine Mind. [10] "And the river, the Merrimac," Kerouac writes, "that roiled huge and floody down past the shrub banks and then spilled a quarter mile broad over the old Indian Falls of Pawtucket and smoshed in the smooth rocks and rambled and made white mysterious pools and dark ones and then gurgled like a huge throat through the slaty rocks deep in the riverbed and under bridges and around mills and homes and around the vast lake like basin so celebrated in Thoreau's A WEEK ON THE CONCORD AND MERRIMAC and finally went seaward like a symbol, or rather like a river, of people, Back to the Bright Origin Nothingness Sea, O thanks to You Father of all things." Written in 1955, this meditation on the Merrimac both restates and extends the poetic suggestiveness of the riverine imagery deployed in the opening paragraphs of *The Town and the City* – enlarging the metaphoric implication of the river's journey from a representation of the course of human destiny in the world to a representation of stages in the formation and evolution of the universe from emanation through dissolution and return to the original unmanifest state. This is the highest, furthest metaphysical reach of the river as symbol in Kerouac's writing, but other levels of meaning – encompassed by the ultimate significance of the river image – are to be found elsewhere in the author's work.

"The Concord River flows past her house," recalls an adult Jack Duluoz, narrator of *Maggie Cassidy,* remembering the lost love of his youth, the eponymous Maggie Cassidy. [11]

And thereafter, throughout the novel, Maggie is closely associated with the river. "I see her head bowed in thinking of me, by the river," (41) Duluoz remembers, and later, "Maggie by the river," (122) and "Maggie's river making muds more fragrant in the spring." (147) Duluoz describes her as imbued in body, mind and heart by the river near which she lives: her touch "the sweet lost bemused inward-biting far-thinking deep earth river-mad April caress – the brooding river in her unfathomable springtime thoughts – The dark flowing enriched silty heart." (77) There is in the figure of Maggie something haunting, mythic, something of the eternal and universal female.

In contrast to the precisely organized hourly, daily and weekly schedule followed by the ambitious teenage Jack Duluoz, the Concord River knows another, deeper time. For punctual, hustling, young Duluoz, each hour's obligations and occupations are executed to the minute, his track and field times recorded to the tenth of a second, his appointed meetings with Pauline Cole arranged beneath "the big boxlike clock hanging from the wall of the school," (60) while his wakings and retirings to bed are observed according to his family's "green electric clock." (62)

Meanwhile, the ancient, elemental waters of the Concord flow or freeze or thaw according to the slow sequence of the seasons. The river adapts, its currents adjust, it turns and curves according to the shapes and textures of the landscape, ever following the path of least resistance, advancing invincibly toward its goal. The Concord's even rhythms are of another order to those of urgent townsfolk such as young Jack Duluoz, the river's Tao-like, fluid, "effortless action" a measured, steady process standing in marked opposition to the latter's fervent determination.

Concord River, Lowell, Mass.

Infused as she is with the river's influences, informed by its rhythms and mysteries, when visiting Jack in New York City, Maggie is appalled by the artificial cityscape and its frenetic pace, by Jack's shallow, pretentious friends, and by his inflated ambitions. Appealing to him to return with her to Lowell, in her pleas she invokes the river: "come back to our porch of the river," (184) But in his pursuit of excitement, career, success and wealth, Jack is heedless and unyielding, and so Maggie returns alone to "her river." (187) Forsaking in this way both Maggie and the "still and soft" (31)

Concord River that "bears pale stars" on its night waters, (32) Jack's river now is the "corpse ridden Hudson," (178) presumably awash with the bodies of suicides and dead gangsters, the remains of those, we may say, whose lives were botched or whose fortunes foundered. His decision does not bode well for him. We cannot but perceive that in casting aside Maggie and her river, Jack has broken faith with whatever he most deeply is.

Imagery of the Merrimac River is recurrent, but not prominent in *Visions of Gerard.* [12] The seasonal changes related to the river – autumn wind, winter ice, spring thaw and surge – are described, but remain unobtrusive, serving only subtly to suggest a natural context of mutability and continuity surrounding the tragic human events taking place in the novel. Notable lyrical ruminations on rivers occur, though, in *The Dharma Bums* (1958) and in *Desolation Angels* (1965).

In *The Dharma Bums,* the protagonist Ray Smith, hitch-hiking north through Washington to assume his duties as a lookout with the Forest Service, discovers with delight the Skagit River, its life-giving water, its heart-opening beauty. [13] The river's "dreaming belly" and "pure torrent" (223) attract his eye and mind, while later along the river's banks and in its purling waters he encounters what seems to him a parcel of paradise, a fragment of Eden. The splendours of the Skagit inspire in Smith both awe and calm and move him to lyrical ruminations upon the nature of the self and the world: "It was a river wonderland, the emptiness of the golden eternity ... all ululating visionstuff before my eyes, tranquil and everlasting ... the world was like a dream, like a phantom, like a bubble, like a shadow, like a vanishing dew, like a lightning's flash." (225-226)

Skagit River, Wash.

Again in *Desolation Angels*, after an absence of some months atop his mountain lookout post, the narrator is lifted in spirit by the sight of the Skagit River. [14] While riding in a boat on Ross Lake, he rejoices to see once more "my pure little favorite river of the Northwest," (115) and is inspired to give utterance to a rhapsodic celebration of rivers, proceeding from the Skagit to the rivers of the North American continent and then to the rivers of the world, returning in the end to the Skagit: "Ah all the rivers of America I've seen and you've seen – the flow without end, the Thomas Wolfe vision of America bleeding herself out in the night in rivers that run to the maw sea but then comes upswirls and new births, thunderous the mouth of the Mississippi ... smell of the delta, where Gulf of Mexico middens hers stars and opens up for shrouds of water that will divide as they please in dividable unapproachable passes of mountains where lonely Americans live in little lights – always the rose that flows, thrown by lost but intrepid lovers off fairy bridges, to bleed to the sea, and moisten up sun's works and come back again, come back again – The rivers of America ... and all the starlights dancing on all the wavelets of rivers without end and everywhere in the world never mind America, your Obis and Amazons and Urs I believe and Congoal appurtenant Lake Dam Niles of blackest Africa, and Ganges of Dravidia, and Yangtzes, and Orinocos, and Plates, and Avons and Merrimacs and Skagits – ." (115)

The image of a rose cast into a river occurs both in *On the Road* (12) and *Doctor Sax* (156) and would seem to suggest the course of mortal love (and mortal lives) proceeding through earthly existence bound toward an ultimate merging into the source of all Love and Life. At the same time, in its unending cyclic renewal, the river serves as a metaphor merging the temporal with the eternal. The circular pattern of the narrator's paean to rivers, beginning and ending with the Skagit, corresponds to the wheel-like turning of "the flow without end," the ever-revolving, everlasting natural process that brings rain to rivers and rivers to the sea, where sea water rises as vapour to form clouds, from which rain then falls into rivers.

In *Big Sur,* a middle-aged, damaged Jack Duluoz, wounded in mind and spirit, a man afflicted by alcoholism and anxiety, experiences a succession of vivid encounters with – not a river but a lesser watercourse – a creek in Bixby Canyon, at Big Sur, on the coast of California. [15] At the edge of the continent and at the edge of his sanity, Duluoz seeks relief and healing alone in a wilderness cabin, near which a creek runs, its sounds spreading through the surrounding area. In the course of the account of his sojourn at Big Sur, Duluoz' relation to the creek serves as a kind of seismograph of the state of his psyche.

Upon the foggy night of his arrival at Bixby Canyon, searching in the darkness for the cabin which is to be his refuge, Duluoz is struck with fear at the sound of the creek. "It's screaming like a raging flooded river," (12) he remarks in dismay. Although subsequently, he concedes that the ominous sound is "just water over rocks," (13) the incident prefigures terrors to come.

Through Duluoz' early days of solitude in his forest hermitage, the gurgling creek is a constant presence and a source of comfort to him. He takes pleasure in the creek's "many voices," ranging he says "from the kettledrum basin deep bumpbumps to the little gurgly feminine crickles over shallow rocks, sudden choruses of other singers and voices from the log dam, dibble dabble all night long and all day long, the voices of the creek amusing me so much ... ." (19-20)

He later passes "the most marvellous day" (28) of all his retreat wading in the creek, meticulously engineering a channel of clear water for drinking and cooking. His daylong watery task absorbs and satisfies him to the degree that he is surprised to feel a childlike innocence revive in his mind together with an unaccustomed sense of happiness. It is as if contact with the creek has had a soothing effect on his tattered spirit.

An abrupt turning in Duluoz' relation to the creek occurs when in his precarious psychic state he interprets a minor and common natural event as a dread omen of death: "I remember seeing a mess of leaves suddenly go skittering in the wind and into the creek, then floating rapidly down the creek towards the sea, making me feel a nameless horror even then of 'Oh my God, we're all being swept away to the sea no matter what we know or say or do' – " (36) As Duluoz' fragile, besieged sanity cracks and breaks, the creek assumes in his ravaged mind the role of a demonic adversary. He begins to sense that the water is hostile to him, "wants me to go away," (113) and soon finds that the once pleasant purling of the current has become to his hearing "an endless jabbering of blind nature." (113) He now perceives the hitherto delightful polyphonic voices of the creek as a single screech, and imagines that its water suddenly tastes different to him, as if (he misguidedly suspects) someone had polluted the stream with kerosene.

At the peak of his harrowing delirium, Duluoz conceives the desperate notion that "the creek will give me water that will clear away everything and reassure me forever." (195) When such hoped-for salvation fails to occur, however, he feels "like kicking the creek and screaming." (195) He then concludes that the fiendish babbling sounds of the creek have entered into his head, insidiously deriding and distorting his every thought, and "telling me to die." (201) Although ultimately (and precipitately) Duluoz emerges from his infernal night journey, *Big Sur* records no further exchange with the creek, no concluding reconciliation between the broken man and the forest stream.

Malign, even "monstrous," aspects of moving water have been recognized by Kerouac in earlier writings (particularly in *Doctor Sax)* but never before expressed to such an extreme degree. Clearly, though, in *Big Sur,* the wickedness and destructiveness attributed to Bixby Creek are intrinsic neither to the water itself nor to the locale but rather are to be understood by readers as misperceptions and misbeliefs of a mind imprisoned in its own dark delusions. The narrator's morbid frame of mind with regard to the creek may be seen as a measure of his temporary pathological alienation from all that is sound and meaning-ful within and without himself. In this way, in an inverted manner, a watercourse again provides a primary and vital touchstone of what is good and true.

Elsewhere, dispersed throughout Kerouac's prose, allu-sions to and descriptions of rivers abound: the Guadaloupe, the Palajo, the Potomac, the Klamath and Columbia, the Willamette and the Snake, the Hood, the Dalles, the Yakima, the Madison, Gallatin and Jefferson rivers, the Pasco, Rainy and Brazos, the Tennessee and others. It is the Mississippi River, though, the "Father of Waters," that most deeply impresses itself upon Kerouac's imagination, as can be seen in the passages from *Visions of Cody* and *On the Road* cited above. A further meditative description of the mighty Mississippi appears in a prose piece titled *"The Great Western Bus Ride."* [16]

In this piece, the author's evocation of the Mississippi resonates with reflections on that same vigorous river and with other rivers to be found in other of Kerouac's writings (in his "Rain and Rivers" journal, for instance, and elsewhere)

Bluffs along the Mississippi, La Crosse, Wis.

and is worth quoting at length: "the unknown suckling place of the Mississippi River, the gargantuan secret of America that now in midwinter lay flooded and frozen in cakey inundations over vast acres of ranchland, covered with snow – hints of lush floods to come in the Natchez cobblestones a thousand miles away, hint of loamy plantations doomed to crumble far around the trail of the northwinged Missouri and the old south-plunging Mississippi. This was where it all started, and it started in ice. Somewhere along the line a few miles down from old Three Forks elemental lightning cracks a tree one night and that log meanders restlessly, floating downstream; to Helena, Cascade, Wolf Point, Mandan of the winter snows, Council Bluffs; till above St. Louis where the male Missouri rushes huge muddy floods into the feminine Miss, this Odyssiac log from lonely Montana is carried by wide night-shores to Cairo; there to be joined by twigs from New York State via the Ohio and the Allegheny; and on down, a riven wandering log all water-heavy and sunken and turning over, coming in a wraith of mist and fogshrouds to bump that ferry that plows the brown water from Algiers to New Orleans; all the way thousands of miles of snowdrift to weeping willow till one with the movement of the night and the secret of sleep it floats around the keys where the oceangoing ship like an eternal ferry passes again its strange destiny, and goes out to the Gulf, out to night, sea, eternity, stars. A twig from my home and a log from far Montana – for the rain is the sea coming back, and the river (no lake) is the rain repassing to the sea, draining a part of us, always a part of us; and the log rolls restlessly in the night and never comes back." (36-37)

Evoking a mood of awe mixed with melancholy, Kerouac's lyrical description of the Mississippi from its headwaters to its mouth and into the gulf is informed by a tension and interplay of opposites: separation and unity, loss and renewal, origins and ends. The images of the twig and the log would seem to serve as figurative representations of human life and destiny. Like the log and the twig, in this life we are all subject to forces beyond our ken or control, swept along in time, through bends and curves of fortune, driven toward our inevitable destination, yet there to become transfigured in communion with "eternity, stars." There is in the passage cited above a sense of reverent wonder at the vastness of the land through which the mighty river courses and at the vastness of the sea with which it merges, and a concomitant sense of the tentative place the landscape grants us and of the ultimate insignificance of our human presence among such powers and grandeurs: the unstable and impermanent names we assign to Earth's ancient landscapes, our transient ranches, our "crumbling" plantations, our ships and ferrys ever susceptible to weathers, rust and other enfeebling forces, all our structures and artefacts "doomed," the author says, to vanish, all fugitive, all fleeting in geological time and under the aspect of eternity.

Images of river and log appear once again in Kerouac's short story, "The Rumbling, Rambling Blues." [17] The story is related by an anonymous first person narrator (presumably Jack Duluoz) who is working as a cook and counterman in a railroad diner. He longs, we are told, to resume his travels but lacks the money to do so. "I'd been there too long," (41) he laments, feeling thwarted, but still he hesitates to depart before he is sure he has sufficient money to serve as security. The narrator kindly befriends a wizened and wise "old Negro hobo" (41) who then demonstrates that he can read the narrator's inmost soul. The old hobo senses the predicament of the narrator: the frustration and the yearning to move on, the caution and the ambivalence that have arrested him on his journey and that combine to keep him in place. The hobo accurately diagnoses the narrator's plight and implicitly advises him, saying: "you's a river log ain't rolling," (43) and telling him of logs he's seen on the Mississippi River that get caught in a snag, their journey hindered.

In a passage of the story bearing significant resemblance to similar descriptions in *On the Road* and "The Great Western Bus Ride," the narrator acknowledges the aptness to his situation of the log and river metaphor deployed by the insightful old hobo: "I understood those logs he was talking about – I had seen them from the decks of ships in New Orleans at night, wandering logs all riven, water-heavy, sunken and turning over that come with the Missouri rushing hugely into the floods of the Mississippi all the way from top-big-muddy, which is lonely old Montana in the north, Odyssiac logs, stately wanderers, moving slowly with satisfaction and eternity down wide night shores out to sea." (44) Inspired, then, by the old hobo's wise counsel, with renewed confidence the narrator takes up once again his journey. "I'd never get caught," he vows, "I'd roll far too." (44)

Noteworthy in the section cited above is the author's explicit anthropomorphization of the logs as "wanderers," and as sentient, capable of feeling "satisfaction" in their movement. Clearly, this device invites readers to view the logs as having parallels to human life and serves to re-enforce the old hobo's use of the log metaphor in referring

Log jam in Mississippi River

to the narrator and his current psychological plight. Of interest here, too, is the adjective "Odyssiac" applied to the logs. In earlier descriptions by the author of the journey of logs down the Mississippi River to the gulf, Kerouac deployed much the same term: "Odyssean" logs in *On the Road,* "Odyssiac" logs in "The Great Western Bus Ride."

In comparing the journey of the logs to the long, arduous, adventurous voyage of Odysseus from Troy to his home in Ithaca as told in *The Odyssey* by Homer, Kerouac elevates the logs (and by extension, the narrator) to heroic status, their overcoming of trials and ordeals, obstacles and struggles, in the course of their travels – a triumph of endurance and perseverance.

With his decision to move on, the narrator recovers from his temporary spell of inertia and assumes again the attitude of trust, hope and belief that is implicit in motion, consenting to follow again his destined direction, allowing himself to be – as it were – carried onward by the current, drawn forward by the sea. (I am reminded here of Matthew Arnold's poem, "The Buried Life," where the poet speaks of an epiphanic instant in life when "A man becomes aware of his life's flow/ ... And then he thinks he knows/ The hills where his life rose,/ And the sea where it goes.") In this way, the river in "The Rumbling, Rambling Blues" may be seen to represent the preordained course of our lives, human destiny both collective and individual, the fate which in mysterious fashion we somehow shape with our consent.

In Kerouac's later writings, images of rivers serve as metaphoric contrasts to human hubris and destructiveness. Such a device occurs in the "Introduction" that Kerouac wrote to Robert Frank's *The Americans.* [18] Here, the author writes of "the crazed voyageur of the lone automobile [who] presses forth his eager insignificance." (21) Isolated in his cocoon of metal and glass, the unattentive driver is oblivious to the natural splendours through which he speeds, and remains wilfully ignorant of the tremendous forces that have formed them. (And of the Force behind those forces.)

Among the wonders of nature Kerouac catalogues – wonders that ought otherwise to have evoked in the impercipient driver amazement and reverence – are rivers such as the Little Missouri, the Ohio, the "Big Muddy" (21) and the Yellowstone.

In a corresponding manner, in a travel essay titled "On the Road to Florida," a river image is employed by the author as an exemplar of natural virtue, an innocent entity remote from the obsessions and transgressions of the frantic inhabitants of the continent. [19] On his automobile journey south from New England to Florida, Kerouac notes across the once untouched American landscape the endless highways with their countless cars and trucks, the road stands and roadside diners, the gas stations and motels, the billboards and the junkyards, and the sites of long ago battles. Crossing the Potomac River on a bridge, he reflects that "the waters roll on anyway, mindless of America's mad invention." (26) Indifferent to the uproar of self-important humanity, Nature calmly pursues its own aims and ends.

Similarly, in his final published piece, "What Am I Thinking About?" a river is used to emphasize by contrast the human and the natural realms of the earth. [20] Kerouac first conveys his strong disapproval of and alienation from nearly every aspect of contemporary life: business executives, politicians, political radicals, psychedelic proselytizers, Marxists and their minions. With regard to the protracted and ongoing war in Vietnam, he laments the killing of civilians and the misery and misfortune visited on innocents by both parties in the conflict. In contrast to the chaos and waste of the war, Kerouac observes: "The Mekong, it's just a long, soft river." (187) The Mekong River here (like the Potomac River in the passage cited above) exemplifies an order of life indifferent to ideologies and national boundaries, a discrete, peaceful domain beyond empires and governments, military victories or defeats. Calmly, quietly, the ancient venerable river makes its way from Tibet through China, Myanmar, Thailand, Laos, Cambodia and Vietnam to the sea. The implication here would seem to be that humankind would do well to allow itself to be instructed by the silent counsel and tranquil example offered by the river.

I would not wish to draw too close a correspondence, but parallels may be seen between rivers and Kerouac's spontaneous prose technique. Kerouac favours in his writing long sentences; compound-complex, extended, winding verbal watercourses. As far as possible, he eschews standard punctuation, preferring the em dash to sustain an unbroken outpouring of words. Borne forward by rhythm and sound, his sentences have their currents and cascades, their rapids and meanders. He often invents onomatopoeic neologisms in imitation of the sounds of moving water: *wush, sprawsh, oom oom zooooo, raw-roar-roo, smosh, dibble, dabble, lappling* and *gabbing*. River imagery also occurs in the author's descriptions of his own work methods, as for example in his personal literary manifesto, *Essentials of Spontaneous Prose*. [21] Here, Kerouac commends the "undisturbed flow from the mind" of words and images, (69) and describes the narrative structure of the prose work over which the flow of language must run as "river rock." (70) Similarly, in *Belief & Technique for Modern Prose,* [22] he refers to "the flow that already exists intact in mind" (72) that must be channelled by the writer. I note, too, that in *Statement on Poetics,* [23] in describing how poetry can be written, Kerouac advises: "add alluvials to the end of your line," (76) thus suggesting that poetic composition is itself like a river.

Elsewhere in his writings, Kerouac acknowledges the link between the flow of his words onto the page and water moving in a river. In *Doctor Sax,* in an aside, the narrator recognizes such a connection, remarking: "Deep in myself I'm mindful of the action of the river, in words that sneak slowly like the river, and sometimes flood ....." (162) And, again, in *The Subterraneans,* [24] the narrator likens the rush of inspiration in literary composition to a river within: "the visions of great words in rhythmic order all in one giant archangel book go roaring thru my brain ... the flow of the river sounds, words, dark ....." (42)

During more than twenty years of literary writing, Jack Kerouac was repeatedly drawn to riverine imagery as a potent and evocative motif. Among the various texts and contexts in his oeuvre in which such images appear, there is both a convergence and a collision of meanings. Rivers are depicted by the author as various and contradictory in their import. They are benign and destructive, noble and fearful. They offer freedom and adventure but may also occasion danger and destruction of property and life. Their serene beauty lifts the spirit; their might and their wrath inspire awe. They can serve both to express an image of the preconscious mind and of a posthumous state of pure being, of oneness with all that exists. They can signify individual fate and collective human destiny. They are seen to embody a primal purity and to have been sullied and desecrated by heedless humans. They are seen to represent both transience and continuity, both the end of life and its eternal renewal.

Clearly, the river image in Kerouac's work points beyond itself in diverse ways. Ultimately, I believe, this complex and paradoxical image even points beyond its multiple meanings. Taken together, in all its array of variations, Kerouac's riverine imagery seems to me to suggest an underlying intuition of some formidable primal force beyond appearances, an unknown, unfathomable level of existence in which opposites meet and divisions are reconciled. More than merely a metaphor, rivers were for the author a manifestation of the numinous, a manifestation of a force fundamental and ultimate, a force that transcends what it inhabits. In the rivers that so haunted and humbled him, Kerouac understood that he confronted something that speaks of a Mystery which no words can compass, a Power, ineffable and unnameable, calling forth in him an awe and a reverence that found expression in some of the most vividly visual and lyrical passages in his writing.

NOTES

1 "Biographical Resumé, Fall 1957" in *Heaven and Other Poems* by Jack Kerouac, Grey Fox, Bolinas, California: 1977, p. 39.

2 *The Town and the City* by Jack Kerouac, Harcourt, Brace & Co. New York: 1950, p. 3. Parenthetical page references hereafter are to this edition.

3 *Windblown World, The Journals of Jack Kerouac 1947-1954,* ed. by Douglas Brinkley, New York: Viking, 2004, p. 198.

4 *Ibid.* p. 281.

5 http://marionblackburn.net/Kerouac/road_ms_med,jpg

6 *On the Road* (1957) by Jack Kerouac, New York: Viking, 1957. Parenthetical page references are to Penguin Classics Edition, London & New York: 2003.

7 *Visions of Cody* by Jack Kerouac, New York: McGraw-Hill, 1972. Parenthetical page references hereafter are to Flamingo edition, London: Grafton Books, 1992.

8 *Book of Sketches* by Jack Kerouac, London & New York: Penguin Books, 2006. Parenthetical page references hereafter are to this edition.

9 *Doctor Sax* by Jack Kerouac, New York: Grove Press, 1959. Parenthetical page references hereafter are to this edition.

10 *Some of the Dharma* by Jack Kerouac. New York: Viking Press, 1997, p. 355.

11 *Maggie Cassidy* by Jack Kerouac, New York: Avon Books, 1959. Parenthetical page references hereafter are to this edition.

12 *Visions of Gerard* by Jack Kerouac, New York: Farrar, Straus & Company, 1963.

13 *The Dharma Bums* (1958) by Jack Kerouac, London: Penguin Books, 1986. Parenthetical page references hereafter are to this edition.

14 *Desolation Angels* (1965) by Jack Kerouac, London: Paladin Grafton Books, 1990. Parenthetical page references hereafter are to this edition.

15 *Big Sur* by Jack Kerouac, New York: Farrar Strauss & Cudahy, 1962. Parenthetical page references hereafter are to this edition.

16 "The Great Western Bus Ride" by Jack Kerouac, *Esquire,* March 1970. Reprinted in *Good Blonde & Others* by Jack Kerouac, San Francisco: Grey Fox Press, 1993. Parenthetical page references hereafter are to this edition.

17 "The Rumbling, Rambling Blues" by Jack Kerouac, *Playboy,* January 1958. Reprinted in *Good Blonde and Others.* Parenthetical page references hereafter are to this edition.

18 "Introduction" by Jack Kerouac to *The Americans: Photographs by Robert Frank,"* New York: Grove Press, 1960. Reprinted in *Good Blonde & Others.* Parenthetical page references hereafter are to this edition.

19 "On the Road to Florida" by Jack Kerouac, *Evergreen Review,* January 1970. Reprinted in *Good Blonde & Others.* Parenthetical page references hereafter are to this edition.

20 "What Am I Thinking About?" by Jack Kerouac, published as "After Me, the Deluge" in *Chicago Tribune Magazine,* September 28, 1969. Reprinted in *Good Blonde & Others.* Parenthetical page references hereafter are to this edition.

21 "Essentials of Spontaneous Prose" by Jack Kerouac, *Black Mountain Review,* Autumn, 1957. Reprinted in *Good Blonde & Others.* Parenthetical page references hereafter are to this edition.

22 "Belief & Technique for Modern Prose" by Jack Kerouac, *Evergreen Review,* Spring 1959. Reprinted in *Good Blonde & Others.* Parenthetical page references hereafter are to this edition.

23 "Statement on Poetics" by Jack Kerouac, *The New American Poetry,* New York: Grove Press, 1960. Reprinted in *Good Blonde & Others.* Parenthetical page references hereafter are to this edition.

24 *The Subterraneans* by Jack Kerouac, New York: Grove Press, 1958. Parenthetical page references hereafter are to this edition.